For Love and Money
Starting and Running a Professional Pet Sitting Business

By
Sonja Red Bird Clay

To Steve; how did I ever get so lucky? And to Diane, for sharing "The Lump" with me, and for always making me smile.

For Love and Money
Starting and Running a Professional Pet Sitting Business

Table of Contents

Insurance
Communications
Computer, Software, Printer
Website
Office Supplies

Chapter Four
Making the Phone Ring ------------------------------------37
Marketing, Advertising, and P.R.

What is the Difference?
Marketing Strategies
P.R.
Advertising that Works

Chapter Five
Interviewing for the Job------------------------------------49
The "Meet and Greet"

Presentations that POP (be Prepared, Organized, and
Professional)
What to Expect
Collecting all Pertinent Information

Chapter Six
Great! You're Hired. Now What? ----------------------57
Preparing for the Sit

What to Do Each Visit
Feed/Water
Mail, Blinds and Lights
Plant Care
Housekeeping
Pet care routine

Apartment Move-in Coupon

Administrative Materials
Monthly Profit/Loss Spreadsheet
3 Year Profit/Loss Spreadsheet
Correspondence
Leasing Agent Letter
Apartment Locator Letter
Realtor Letter
Brochure Request Response Letter
Collection Letter

SBA
PUPS
NAPPS
PSI
PSA
Online Pet Sitting Listings
Search Engine Submissions
Office Supplies
Printing Services
Free Online Computer Program Tutorials

Introduction

In the fall of 2005, I began a wonderful adventure. After spending much too much time in a stressful work environment, I threw caution to the wind and, in a huge leap of faith, gave up a good salary to begin Spot Check Pet Services. The success of the business surprised even me. Within 6 months my husband was able to leave his full time job and join me in spending our days caring for some of the sweetest pets in the world! The rewards have been great, and we have never looked back.

The information contained in this book is the result of personal experience. The practices are based on what has worked best for Spot Check Pet Services, and were arrived at through trial and error.

It is my sincere hope that this information will be of help to you in starting and growing your own successful pet sitting business, and that you may benefit from what I have learned "the hard way." The resources listed at the end of the book, although by no means exhaustive, have been very useful tools in our business development.

Best of luck to you and happy pet sitting!

Chapter One

The Truth about Cats and Dogs
Dispelling Myths and Misunderstandings

There are many misconceptions regarding the pet sitting industry. Let's begin by examining a few of them and setting the record straight.

Myth: Anyone can be a pet sitter. The kid down the street does it.

Truth: Yes, anyone can *call* themselves a pet sitter, just as anyone can call themselves just about anything. But to be a professional pet sitter, you must do many things that the kid down the street is not doing. You must maintain insurance. You must educate yourself continually on pet care. You must be dependable, reliable and professional. And, most of all, you Must Love Pets!

Myth: Pet sitting is easy work.

Truth: Pet sitting will get you out of bed at 6 a.m. on a Saturday morning. Pet sitting will get you home at 9 or 10 p.m. that same day. You will be called upon to clean up all manner of animal "messes." Accidents do happen, and usually will happen during *your* watch! Some pets require your physical exertion, such as the giant happy Lab puppy that needs 4 brisk walks a day. You will be out in the rain, heat, cold, and snow if your area gets it. Cats can be very unfriendly and do not necessarily appreciate strangers in their homes. They can make your job difficult if they are so inclined. You will work 7 days a week, and twice as much on holidays. Every Holiday.

Myth: I can get rich quick pet sitting.

Truth: Oh how I wish that one was true! You will not become an overnight millionaire by pet sitting. With that said, it is possible to earn a living wage by pet sitting. Some sitters do quite well, and hire others to grow and expand their business. The bottom line is that you will get out of your business exactly what you put into it. If you approach pet sitting with a positive mindset and focus on growing your company, you will be financially successful.

Myth: I can start a successful pet sitting business without investing any money into it.

Truth: Um, no. Although you can start a pet sitting business with very little capital, there are expenses to consider. The old adage "It takes money to make money," is true in all circumstances. You can begin your business on a "shoestring," but you will need to invest in advertising, marketing materials, office supplies, insurance, and association fees if you choose to join any.

Myth: I don't need to commit to pet sitting. It's not like it's a "real job." I can just do it when I feel like it, or need a little spending cash.

Truth: No, no, and no! Professional pet sitting is a commitment in itself. Pet sitters rely on their reputation as dependable professionals to succeed. Clients will call you to care for their pets when they travel on weekends and holidays. If you are fortunate enough to develop a daily dog walking route, those clients count on you to make sure their pets receive daily visits, regardless of your personal plans. You must approach your business with a serious, professional attitude if you want to build your client base and your reputation. Offering "spotty" service makes a would-be pet sitter no more professional than the kid down the street.

Like all endeavors, there are pros and cons to professional pet sitting. The pros outweigh the cons for all professional sitters; otherwise we would not be doing it! Entering the business with realistic expectations will help you to remain positive and feel comfortable that you are on the right track when doubts try to creep in. Let's start with the down side of pet sitting, and then take a look at the benefits. Then you will be able to decide for yourself if pet sitting is really for you.

The Cons:
Unless you truly love animals and have a passion for providing top rate customer service, you will not be happy pet sitting. Much of a pet sitter's day is spent driving. You will be out in all weather conditions. You will be called upon to work all holidays and weekends. Unless you have a good support system in place, the possibility of "burn-out" is very real. There is very little human interaction during the usual course of a pet sitter's day. Pets will drool on you, "pee" on you, scratch you, shed on you, jump on you with muddy paws, and otherwise dirty you; and that's assuming they like you!

The Pros:
Pets in your care will greet you with joyful enthusiasm every time they see you. They will give you unconditional love and friendship. You will be your own

boss, with all of the freedom that comes with it. Caring for pets and providing pet owners with peace of mind brings great personal satisfaction. You can choose your business practices based on what works best for you. You will not be cooped up in a stuffy building for 8 hours every day. You will get lots of exercise and fresh air, and be paid to do it. You will meet many interesting and wonderful people and pets. No two days are ever the same, so there is little chance for boredom.

If this sounds like a fair trade off to you, then prepare for a fantastic journey into the wonderful world of professional pet sitting and read on!

> The most difficult thing for me has been the lack of days off. We haven't been able to step away from the business for more than 3 concurrent days in the last four years. While I love the pets we care for, and it's hard to call spending time with them "work," there is a lack of balance in our lives at this point.
>
> The thing that keeps me from hiring or subcontracting work is the fear that sits won't be done to my standards, and that our client relationships will suffer for it. I know that there are many pet sitters that have great success using outside help, but it's hard for me to let go.
>
> I love spending time with the dogs that we see every day for walks, and look forward to seeing them. I'm very attached to them all, and miss them when they go on vacation or take a day off. They are the bright spot to any day!

Chapter Two

Getting the Ball Rolling
First Steps to Setting up Your Business

Now that you know the truth about cats and dogs, and have decided that pet sitting is indeed for you, it's time to make some decisions about your business. The first thing you need to decide on is the business structure that works best for you. There are 4 types of business structures to consider.

1. Sole Proprietorship- According to the Small Business Administration, most businesses begin as sole proprietorships. This is the most simple business structure. The benefits are that it is the least expensive type of company to form, the owner keeps or reinvests all revenue as he or she sees fit, and control is maintained by the sole proprietor. The drawback is that the owner is legally responsible for all debts and liabilities incurred by the business. Their business, as well as personal assets are at risk.
2. Partnership-Partnerships are very similar to sole proprietorships; with the exception that more than one person owns the business. Partnership agreements must be made to cover decision making, profit sharing, and all aspects of the business.
3. Limited Liability Company or LLC- The LLC is beneficial for small businesses because it combines the limited personal liability feature of a corporation with the tax advantages of a partnership and sole proprietorship. Profits and

losses can be passed through the company to its members or the LLC can choose to be taxed like a corporation.

4. Corporation-Corporations are complex business structures that have many more start up costs than other structures. A corporation is considered a separate entity from owners, so owners have much more protection financially if anything should go wrong. Corporations are taxed at a different (possibly higher) rate than other forms of business.

There are benefits to each type of business, and only you can know which structure is right for you. The good news is that you can restructure your sole proprietorship, partnership, or LLC if you decide that incorporation is the way to go.

> When I set Spot Check Pet Services up, I chose to go with a sole proprietorship. It was very easy to do. In Bexar County, Texas, a sole proprietorship requires a D.B.A., which can be obtained at the county court house. The clerk researches the name to insure no other business is already registered under that name. I filled out a short form and took a trip to a notary public, and then, after a return visit to the clerk along with a small fee, viola! Spot Check Pet Services was now legitimate and legal.

Business Plan

The next step is to make a business plan. A business plan is like a road map to your destination. It is the tool that will tell you if your business is on course.

Business plans can be very simple statements jotted down on a piece of paper or detailed formal documents many pages long. The best business plan is one that allows you to put your vision, mission, and goals down. Your business plan can be requested when seeking outside funding and loans, in which case, a more formal plan can be of benefit.

There are many templates available for business plans (see resources), or if the notion of writing your plan seems too daunting, you can always hire someone to write it for you. Ideally, your plan will change and grow as your business does. Think of it as a living document, always evolving to meet your current needs. Don't be afraid of your plan. Embrace it as your friend and use it to help guide your way.

> There was a lot of helpful information online, and I'm not sure I could have done it without it! The SBA has many free resources for business start-ups, and their business plan template helped me to write mine.

Choosing a Name

One of the most fun parts of starting your new business is picking a name that will stand out in a crowd, give an indication of what your business offers (i.e. pet sitting), and allow you to creatively express your individuality.

Think of some of the business names that you have seen or heard. Do any of them stand out in your mind? What was it about them that caught your eye? Now, think of some names that instantly "turned you off." What was it about them that rubbed you wrong? The name of your business is an essential part of your overall business image. Keep this in mind if you are tempted to use any colorful metaphors or inappropriate plays on words. While they may get an occasional giggle, you may be projecting the wrong image to potential customers.

Don't be tempted to give your business a name that puts it at the top of the alphabetical listing in the phone book. While AAAA Amazing Pet Sitting may show up first in line, it may not catch the eye of people searching for a pet sitter. Besides that, think of how you'll sound answering your phone, "A-a-a-a amazing pet sitting, how I can help you?" Your caller may simply assume that you have a terrible stutter.

Once you have an idea about what you might like to call your business, and you've conducted the proper "phone test" mentioned above, it's time to research your name. Make sure that there are no other businesses using your chosen name. A good way to do this is to do an internet search of the name and see if anything comes up. Keep in mind that if a business does not have a web presence, it won't come up in your online search. Also, you'll need to check with your local courthouse, especially if you decide to get a D.B.A. as a sole proprietor.

You may also like to think of a tag line or company motto that flows well with the name of your business. Try saying them out loud to get a feel for what they will sound like together. Tag lines are another part of your company image, or branding. The same rules apply to tag lines as to names. Make sure not to inadvertently offend or project a negative image.

Picture your name and tag line on your marketing materials. You'll want it to be short enough to fit on your business cards. Consider your web address as well. You don't want to have a website based on your business name that is too long or difficult to remember.

> I had the name Spot Check in mind for some time. I thought it was quirky and catchy, and the visual it brought to mind seemed like the perfect logo. I "Googled" the name first, and found no other pet companies using it; so that's the name we went with. It does make for a very long web address, and even longer e-mail. I didn't think of that at the time!

D.B.A., Licensing, and More

Taking your newly chosen business name to the proper registering and licensing bodies is very exciting. All counties and states have different regulations regarding businesses within their jurisdiction. Make sure you research the requirements thoroughly before going any further. You can usually find most information online, or by contacting the appropriate local government agencies.

You will also need to look into local tax requirements. Many areas require sales tax registration. Again, your internet research and/or phone skills will help you dot all your i's and cross all your t's.

For other business structures, such as a corporation or LLC, or to produce a legal partnership agreement, you may need to enlist the help of an attorney. It is a wise idea to have an attorney look over any documents or forms that you may have filled out yourself as well. Sometimes as few as one or two words will make all the difference somewhere down the road.

Banking

Banks are businesses. They want to earn your patronage. Some banks offer great perks to their customers, and some do not. Some have fantastic customer service, and sadly, some do not. You will want to choose a bank that is the best fit for both you and your business needs.

Don't be afraid to ask questions of your potential banking partners. You'll be glad you did your research should anything out of the ordinary come up. Also ask any other small business owners about their banking experiences before making your decision. Remember, although you can always change banks if you find your current one is not meeting your needs, it can be slightly inconvenient at best.

Some questions to ask include:
- What fees are associated with a business account?
- What is the minimum balance?
- Do you offer any special services to small business owners?
- Do you offer lines of credit to account holders?
- Are there any benefits to one type of account over another?
- What are your out of town check policies?
- Do you offer online banking?

Other considerations should be:
- What are the banking hours?
- Are there branches located conveniently to you?
- Are there ATM machines available for transactions after hours?

- Are friendly tellers available to assist you?
- Do you like the "feel" of the bank itself?

Once you choose your ideal bank, you'll need your business documentation, along with your personal identification and social security card to open your account. Now you have a place to put all of those checks that start rolling in!

After setting up my D.B.A., I opened up a business account with the bank we had been using for our personal accounts. I didn't think to ask too many questions, being so new at business ownership. Fortunately, we didn't have too many problems with the service. There were a few instances in which I felt I would've been better served using a more business friendly bank, but over all it's been ok. I did look into moving our account at one point, but decided against it when I found out that our balance would have to remain in "bank limbo" for a period of time without having access to it.

Chapter Three

Setting up Shop
What You Need to Begin

Great! Your foundation work is done, and now you are ready to get down to the business of running your business! This is where the serious work begins. You are going to need a few things to start with. This is just a basic list that you may want to add to as you go along. We did say that pet sitting could be started on a shoestring, so cost effective methods will be discussed here as well as some slightly pricier options.

Decide on the Types of Jobs You Like to Do

Now is the time to take a moment and decide which type of work will suit you best. If you haven't already done so, consider your availability and preferences.

Do you like working split shifts? Does early morning and late evening work fit into your otherwise busy schedule? If so, you may enjoy working mostly dog sitting assignments. This can be perfect if you are a student, or currently have another job.

The typical dog sitting schedule includes a morning visit, followed by an evening visit. Some pet owners also request additional visits throughout the day, so be sure of your availability before committing to these sits.

Do you prefer to sleep in and be home early? If this is your ideal schedule, then daily dog walking jobs might be the way to go. Dailies also work well with the dog sitting schedule, so that you can do both if you like.

Daily dog walks are usually scheduled somewhere between 11 am and 2 pm on week days. This schedule also works well for parents of school aged children. A big perk to dailies is that you develop a wonderful relationship with the dogs, as you see them every day.

Do you require more flexibility in your schedule? Specializing in cat sitting might be the way to go. Cats typically only require one visit per day, and owners tend to be more flexible about the scheduling of these visits. There are exceptions, of course. Some cats require two or more visits for health reasons, so discuss scheduling these visits thoroughly when you meet with clients.

Other things to consider are the types of pets you enjoy caring for and are comfortable with. If you have a fear of reptiles or rodents, you'll want to steer clear of any jobs involving these creatures!

Policies and Procedures

Now that you've decided what kinds of pet sitting jobs you prefer, you can set your company policies. Having standardized policies and procedures in place will save you a million headaches down the line. It is the cheapest tool in your pet sitting toolbox. All it will cost you is your time and brain power.

It's very difficult to think of every eventuality and come up with company policies to deal with them, so be prepared to evolve your practices as you learn and experience more. Here are some of the more common things to address, just to help you get started. Every company is different and what works for one organization may not work for others.

Payments
- What forms of payment will you accept? Will you be set up to receive cash, check, Pay Pal, or credit cards?
- When is payment due?
- Will you require a deposit for holding advance reservations?
- What late fees will you require?
- Will you charge cancellation fees, and if so, how much?
- Will you charge mileage or travel time fees?
- What will your rates be?
- Will you charge to pick up and drop off keys?
- Will you have a holiday surcharge?
- Will you charge extra for additional animals?

Services
- What services will you offer?
- What area of town will you service?
- Are there any animals that you feel you couldn't care for?

Time off/ Coverage
- Will you take any holidays off?
- How will you cover your customer's needs while you're away?
- Do you have a plan in place should you become sick or injured?
- What will you do in the event of a personal emergency?
- What if you lock your keys in your car?
- What if your car breaks down?

Pets

- How will you handle unruly or biting animals?
- What will you do in case of a pet medical emergency?
- What will you do if a pet in your care becomes injured?
- How will you handle pet damage to the client's home, either by mischief or illness?

Homes

- What will you guarantee in your service agreement?
- What will you do in the event of a burglary?
- What will you do in the event of a fire, flood, or other catastrophe?
- What if you lose the clients key?
- Will you care for plants during your sit?

Once you have outlined your services and policies, you will be able to plan your business better, and use this information to create your business forms and contracts.

> One of the biggest mistakes I made the first year was trying to cover a service area that was just too big. We had work on every side of town and spent hours driving from stop to stop throughout the day.
> Although we made good money that year, after gas and travel time were factored in, our earnings were hardly over minimum wage. After our first tax filing, it became clear that we would have to change our practices.

The hardest part of making that change was letting clients go. Some left through attrition, but others had to be actively let go. We had a good relationship with those clients, and had come to love the pets very much. I did try to offer information on other sitters in their areas, and gave them plenty of advance notice, but it still seemed like we ended up stepping on a few toes.

My advice to anyone thinking of starting a pet sitting business is to get a map. Use the map legend to determine the actual miles from your home or office, and using a compass, circle an area not larger than 10 miles around your base of operation. If you live in a small town or rural setting, you may need to travel further. If you are willing to go 15 miles out (a long way in our experience) then you'll have to come 15 miles back in. That makes a 30 mile round trip. Or, if you have a sit at the east end of your 10 mile radius, and another at the far west end, you will have traveled 10 miles out, 20 miles across and another 10 miles back in. Forty miles for two sits done twice daily racks up the mileage very fast.

Forms

Professional looking forms serve many functions. They allow you to collect information in an organized way. They present a professional company image. They give added peace of mind to prospective clients. Best of all, they will help you feel more confident during your first client meetings. You will be certain that you have collected all important information on your customers and their pets.

Professionally created forms are available for purchase starting at under $40 for a full set, and I highly recommend them (see resources). Some associations also provide forms free of charge to their members. The best ones are fully customizable with your company logo and information. During the first few months of being in business, I found them invaluable for getting me through "meet and greets." They helped me stay focused and on task during meetings, and customers often commented on how professionally I handled the business. The purchase of these forms was a minor investment, and the bonus benefits that came with them have continued to be a tremendous value to the business.

If you are handy with word processing programs, you may want to create your own forms. With your policies and procedures in hand you can generate the necessary paperwork using MS Word, Publisher, Open Office or any other programs you feel comfortable with. If you do decide to create your own contracts, review by a qualified attorney is highly advisable.

Some useful forms to consider are:
- Pet Information Forms
- Veterinary Release Forms
- Home Guides
- Contact Information Sheets
- Contracts
- Invoices
- Receipts
- Sit Logs
- Surveys
- Scheduling and Routing Sheets

Avoid redundant questions on your forms, and design them to be laid out in an organized manner. They should be clear, concise, and thorough. Branding should also be reflected in your forms. This will set you apart from less professional sitters, like the poor kid down the street we keep mentioning.

The policies of our company were arrived at after doing an incredible amount of research and reading. I was very lucky to be browsing the web when I came across the P.U.P.S. site. For $34 I bought the forms offered, and with them came a lifetime membership to Professional United Pet Sitters. Membership includes access to a ton of resources, directory listing, and best of all, the P.U.P.S. forum. The forum is full of incredible sitters who give freely of their advice and experience as well as offer support to members. I can't say enough about this group!

Insurance

If you purchase nothing more for your business, you must buy a reasonable pet sitting insurance policy. This will probably be your largest investment to start with, but it is well worth it! A good policy covers key loss, dog bites, and some injuries to pets in your care. There are also optional additional riders available that act as a bond in the event of mysterious disappearance or breakage of client property.

Carrying sufficient pet sitting insurance will put you in the professional category much more than anything else you can do. Potential clients will often ask if you are bonded and insured, and request proof of coverage.

You wouldn't want to drive your car without liability insurance; don't operate your business without it! This is especially important for sole proprietors and partnerships in order to avoid any personal financial loss should something unforeseen happen.

There are several insurance providers that offer pet sitting insurance. The prices and benefits are listed in the resources section to help you choose the best coverage for your business.

If you will have a spouse or employees working with you, you will need to look into the policy coverage for them as well. You will want anyone that represents your company to be insured.

I chose to go with Pet Sitters Associates for our insurance. It was the least expensive, offered great coverage, and didn't have any prerequisites requiring us to belong to any pricy associations. We've never filed a claim, but I have read of others doing so with no problems. Having the insurance gives me great peace of mind.

Communications

How will your customers get in contact with you? Do you prefer a land line with an answering machine for when you're away, or a cell phone which you can keep with you and take calls at any time?

The benefits of a cell phone are portability, ease of set-up, and cost effectiveness. Cell phones offer built in features such as phone number storage, caller id, text capability, voice mail, and even cameras. You can answer your cell phone throughout the day while away from your office. There are prepaid services that allow you to buy only the minutes needed, so you can control your bill effectively.

One of the biggest drawbacks to using a cell phone as your primary telephone is the quality of reception you may encounter. Depending on your area, and the phone service you choose, you may experience dropped calls, static on the lines, difficulty connecting, and other quality issues. Cell phones can also be easily lost or broken.

Land lines can be a good option if you have a home office and plan to have someone answer the phone while you are out pet sitting. You can set up a second phone line for very little cost. The quality of connection is vastly superior using a land line. You can use an answering machine to receive calls while you are away, or subscribe to call notes if available in your area.

The down side to land lines is that you will be unable to give immediate response to your clients. If you have a noisy home office this could come across as very unprofessional to potential customers. Also, you must be certain that anyone answering the business line is very professional and polite to callers. Unfortunately, even the most polite child with perfect phone etiquette should not answer your business phone. Land lines are not as easily transferred should you wish to set up your office elsewhere later. Changing your business number could cause clients to have a hard time getting in touch with you.

Consider where you'd like your business to be in a year, or two, or more when you set up your phone service. While changing your number down the road is not impossible, you will need to change your advertisements, marketing materials, business cards, and notify your existing client base should you choose to do so.

My business cell phone has been our means of communication from the beginning. I decided to use a prepaid service to make the phone more transferable should we ever need to pass the number along. Virgin Mobile offered all the features I needed at a very reasonable price. There are many prepaid and contract cell phone service providers out there, and it can save you a mint if you do a little research before committing. I've been very pleased with our service overall.

There were a few instances when our cell phone was in jeopardy from big, enthusiastic pets. In the end, I did away with the belt clip portion of the phone, as it was somehow very attractive to them. Keeping the phone charged and ready to go at all times can be a challenge without a car charger. A headset is also a great investment; but again, watch out for big dogs that see it as a cool chew toy, or try to rescue you from that strange thing on your head!

Computer, Software, and Printer

You don't actually *need* a computer to start your pet sitting business, but it will make your life much easier if you do have one! You will be able to customize your forms, create your fliers, brochures, business cards, website, client database, and spreadsheets much easier if you have access to a computer with either open office or Microsoft Office Suite on it.

You also will need a computer to respond to e-mail sent by clients. Many busy professionals who don't have the time for a phone call somehow find a moment to send a quick e-mail to their pet sitters during the day.

You can purchase a relatively inexpensive used computer and printer without breaking the bank. It doesn't need to be an extraordinary machine to get the job done. It is a business investment that will pay for itself very quickly.

For those of you who are confirmed technophobes, fear not! Today's computers and software programs are very user friendly. There are also many classes offered to teach new computer users how to find their way around their p.c.s. Some libraries even offer free computer classes.

You will also need an internet connection to allow you to send and receive e-mail, set up and maintain your website, participate in online pet sitting message boards, and perform the necessary business research to build and grow your business.

A printer will round out your office set-up nicely. With a desktop printer you can generate all of your marketing

materials "in house." This will save you a ton of money!
Instead of relying on outside companies for your printing
needs-- which is very costly-- you can print small
amounts of materials as needed.

As for a computer, Spot Check Pet Services was
created and launched using an old p.c. that we
lovingly refer to as the "old man." It has less power
than a PlayStation 2, but it is still in service keeping us
running. We do all of our invoicing, bookkeeping, and
printing with this computer, and it has never let us
down. It was purchased used in 2001, so it's basically
an antique where technology is concerned.

The software we use is Microsoft Office Suite. There
are a few programs specifically designed for the pet
care industry, but I can do everything I need to with
Office. I did download a couple of trial versions of pet
sitting software, but chose not to purchase in the end.
It really depends on your comfort level with software
and computers as to which route you choose to take.
For me, I was familiar with the Office Suite, so it was
easy to apply to our business needs.

Website

In today's marketplace, web presence can make all the
difference between success and failure. This is a
strong statement. However, more and more people are
turning to the internet to receive information. It's easier
to go to your keyboard and type in "pet sitters" than to
drag out the yellow pages, sort through numerous non-
descript listings, and call 2 or three that sound
appealing and ask a series of questions about their
services.

A properly designed website serves several functions. It allows you to showcase your business in a unique and individual way. It serves as a full screen advertisement for your services. It provides relevant information to prospective clients. Most importantly, it provides customers with a means of contacting you via your e-mail link.

Your website should reflect your individual style and make a statement about your pet care philosophies. Before a potential customer ever reads your content, they will make a subconscious decision about you based on the appearance of your website. They will decide if you are a good fit for them and their pets based on the "feel" of the pages.

You can use your website to advertise your business very cost effectively. It allows you to state your customer's pet care needs and tell them how *you* can fill them. The content of your website should be designed to show how your company is the perfect solution to all of their pet care problems. Be specific in what you can do for your clients and their pets. Don't be overly modest here.

Information such as service area, types of services offered, kinds of pets that you care for, pricing, and availability should be included to help pet owners in decision making.

A "contact us" link allows customers to send you an e-mail right from your website. It encourages them to get in touch with you then and there, while you and all of the fine benefits of your services are still fresh in their minds.

You don't need to be a computer programming genius or even have html or java experience to set up your own website. Many web hosts offer easy to use templates to make website design a snap. All you need to do is write your wording and choose the way you want your site to look. Then, follow the easy instructions given by the web host, and you'll be up and running in no time!

Speaking of web hosts, you will need to choose a company to host your site for you. There are tons of web hosts out there, and there are all levels of pricing as well. You can decide which features will work best for your website and make the right choice of host from there.

If you find you wish to change hosts later, it's not terribly complicated. The most important thing to decide is what your domain name will be. A domain name is what appears after "www." and before ".com." Ideally your business name will also be your domain name. This makes it easier for customers to find you online. You can take your domain name with you should you change web hosts in the future.
If your head is spinning and you feel overwhelmed at the mere notion of setting up a website, you can always hire a professional to do it for you. If you decide to do so, ask to see some of their previous work. Also, choose a designer with whom you can work comfortably. Your input and design ideas should be encouraged. After all this is *your* website, and your business image!

> Website building was brand new to me when I designed the Spot Check pages. I had no html experience, and still don't! I chose a hosting company called Doteasy, and it was indeed easy. They offer

templates that can be customized to fit your needs. All I really needed to do was apply the advertising principles that are discussed in the next chapter and it was up and running. It's easy to maintain, and suits our limited needs. If you want to have your forms available online, host a blog or forum, or use a checkout service then you may need a different host. Our website was designed to be strictly informational, so our needs are simple.

I wanted our email to contain our business name. When I look for a service company and see a hotmail, yahoo, gmail, or other free e-mail service listed in their contact info, I tend to wonder about the professionalism of the business. I know that it really has nothing to do with it at all, but subconsciously it just turns me off to a company that doesn't have their own branded e-mail.

Office Supplies

The office supply needs of a pet sitting business are really pretty simple. Depending on your decision regarding a printer, you'll need paper and ink. If you will be doing your own printing, it's a good idea to invest in some heavier paper or specialty paper for your marketing materials. Regular 20 lb white printer paper is fine for forms, invoices, receipts, and notes. Stock up on ink if you plan on doing any substantial amount of printing. Nothing slows you down more than having to run to the store for more ink in the middle of a project.

Standard office supplies such as a stapler, staples, paper clips, file folders, pens, ledger sheets, and such will be needed to run your office.

In addition, a 3 ring binder is very helpful for keeping your routing sheets and information in. You can also use a binder to create your presentation book for use at meetings with clients. Clear plastic sheet protectors work very well for this too.

Office supplies can be ordered online and in bulk if you want. I know many business owners who do so. For me, there is a certain joy in walking into an office supply store and filling my cart with things my business needs. I do always use a list when shopping; otherwise it's easy for me to go way over budget. I like to have a checklist that I can mark things that we need off as we go. There's not a lot of storage space in our home office, so we're strictly on a buy as needed basis.

Chapter Four

Making the Phone Ring
Marketing, Advertising, and P.R.

What is the difference between marketing, advertising, and P.R.? To simplify things for the purpose of this book, we will define them as three separate activities, although advertising and Public Relations technically fall under the category of marketing. All 3 will help bring customers to your business and get your company known. Marketing and P.R., or Public Relations, are often less expensive, and creative ways to get the word out about your service. Advertising usually involves payment for displaying your advertising copy, and is a more direct way to drive customers to you. You'll need to do all 3 if you want to launch a successful campaign to get your company going.

Marketing

Marketing, as defined by Wikipedia, "is an integrated communications-based process through which individuals and communities are informed or persuaded that existing and newly-identified needs and wants may be satisfied by the products and services of others." Or, plainly put, it's the process of convincing others that you have something that they need.

Marketing, for our purposes, is putting your information out there through networking, or through distributing your marketing materials to individuals or groups with whom your target audience interacts. You can also use your marketing materials, such as fliers or brochures to attract customers by placing them in areas pet owners are known to visit, such as dog parks.

Networking can be done in a number of ways. You don't need to be the life of the party to learn effective networking skills. In fact, sincerity will go much further than a gregarious nature when it comes to making new business contacts. Networking can be as simple as stopping in to a vet clinic to say hello and introducing yourself and your business. You can leave a few business cards at your neighborhood groomer, and take some of their cards to pass on as well. You can join a networking group and attend organized networking events. You can just tell everyone you know about your business venture and ask them to let their friends know about your services as well.

Networking is also about what you can offer others. In an ideal networking relationship, you pass on the information of network members or contacts to those who could benefit from their services. Do you have a fantastic hair stylist? You can send business her way, and she can do the same for you. Have a great bank? Ditto. The opportunities to network your business are only limited by your imagination, and the number of people you're willing to introduce your business to.

When we first started out, I spent a lot of time and gas making my rounds to all the local groomers, vet clinics, pet stores, and pet friendly businesses. I followed the advice in a popular pet sitting how-to book to the letter. I must have used my first batch of business cards up in two weeks or less.

I sent letters to travel agents, apartment complexes, realtors, and anyone else I could think of offering finders fees for referrals.

All of this effort netted us precisely zero clients. Ever! No matter how I approached the marketing, it just never did help us gain new clients. I'm not saying that it doesn't work for other sitters. But it did not work for us.

I think the main reason for this was that I wasn't focusing on a small enough area to be successful. In trying to cover the greater part of a large metropolitan area I just spread my marketing efforts way too thinly to be effective. I wish I had known then what I know now!

P.R.

Public Relations, or P.R. is the act of building your business through working with third parties, such as the press, or special interest groups. Speaking engagements, community involvement, writing articles and newsletters for your target audience, press releases, setting up tables or booths at pet related events are all forms of public relations. So we can say that P.R. then, is activity related business promotion through creating a positive business image within your community.

Press releases are often used as promotional tools by new businesses to attract attention to their industry or individual company. If you don't want to attempt writing your own press release, you can find press release templates both free and for purchase online. You can also hire someone to write one for you. A press release could be sent to local papers and radio stations to announce grand openings, business anniversaries, or other business achievements and milestones.

You could also offer up your pet expertise to groups in need of a speaker for pet related events. Since you will be continually educating yourself on the subject of pets, you should be able to find a topic that you feel comfortable speaking about. Do your research and present an accurate and knowledgeable talk and you will inspire confidence in your pet care abilities. Those in attendance will remember you when they or their friends need a pet sitter later.

If you aren't comfortable with public speaking, you can share your knowledge with your target audience via well written articles and newsletters. Many home owner associations are open to publishing brief articles on pet care in their monthly newsletters. In exchange you will be able to list your business contact information at the end of your article. You could create a useful newsletter for your client base. Keep the information concise and interesting. Be careful not to plagiarize other authors writings, and always cite your resources if appropriate.

Another great way to meet potential customers is to participate in local pet related events, such as pet fairs and parades, adoption fairs, pet centered holiday celebrations, and other gatherings of pet lovers. You can often rent a table and offer pet treats, along with brochures or other information on your business. Consider donating a door prize for the event. You could inexpensively put together a nice pet gift basket, and include your business card or brochure in it.

Charity organizations, churches, and public television stations often have fund raising events to which you could donate a gift certificate for your services. It is tax deductible, easy to put together, and will make you feel good! Do specify your service area in the donation statement, or you might find yourself going miles out of your way to honor the certificate later on.

By participating in and contributing to your local community, you build a solid reputation with pet owners and friends of pet owners as a caring, conscientious, and community minded person. These people will be more likely to think of you when they need pet care. Best of all, by being involved in your community, you will meet lots of great people and have tons of fun doing it! It hardly seems like work at all to go out and participate in activities that are enjoyable, but you don't have to feel guilty. You are working on growing a thriving pet sitting business all the while.

I did enjoy participating in local events, and passing out treats and business cards. Our local public TV station has an annual fund raising auction called Blazing Gavels that we donated a series of 3 day pet sitting gift certificates to. It was good exposure to have our name mentioned on local television, and we did see an increase in calls afterwards. We made the mistake of not including our service area in the donation information, so had to travel way out of range to honor the certificates. Driving for over an hour per 30 minute visit [for free] was kind of disheartening, but we survived!

Advertising

Writing ad copy that sells your service is easier than it sounds! There are a few simple principles to keep in mind when you do design your campaign. Remember that we defined marketing as convincing a group that they actually have a need, and then showing them how you can fill this need perfectly for them? That's exactly what you are going to be doing. The first step to successful advertising is to identify your market. Next, you must explore the needs of this group. Finally, you will offer a solution to solve their pet care needs. You will also tell them why your company is the best choice for them by showing how your services and policies match their situation.

To begin your campaign, you'll have to know your target audience pretty well. In our case, pet owners are our pool of potential clients. Some sitters serve a small niche market of one or two types of pet owners, such as cat fanciers, small animal enthusiasts, or those needing daily dog walking. Is there an under-served market in your area? Do you prefer working with a certain type of animal or clientèle? Once you identify your preferred market, do your research! What are the needs of this group? Are there any common interests or circumstances within this group that you can identify with? What do you feel you can offer to this group?

If you prefer to market to the broader pet owning community, that's fine too. Many successful pet sitters offer a variety of services and flexibility to accommodate different types of customers. The most important thing to keep in mind is your own level of comfort. Choose the services that you like to do. As Ben Franklin said,

"If you enjoy what you do, you will never work a day in your life."

Step two in your ad design is to discuss the needs of your target market. Many businesses make the mistake of telling potential clients how great their service or product is without ever telling them what is in it for the client. People want to hear about themselves, not your company. Focus your advertising on the clients needs first. Some marketing experts advise that you present your markets needs in a very sympathetic way.

Let them know that you feel for them. After all, it really is sad that they are forced to leave their beloved dog home alone all day long while they work. You know that they would much rather be home with their pal, right? Travel is so stressful when your best friend is cooped up in a kennel while you are away. It must be so hard to have fun or focus on business meetings knowing that pets had to remain behind.

Once you establish the issues or concerns of your market, tell them how you can solve their problems. You can come give some companionship and exercise to the latch-key dog during the work day! You can provide care right in the pet's home while owners travel! No need to add stress by sending them out to a kennel. You will give attention, t.l.c., top rate care, and keep pets happy when they cannot.

Notice that nowhere in this list of solutions did we say anything about you or your company and services specifically. What we did say is what you can do for your clients. The old adage "sell the sizzle, not the steak" applies to all advertising. What are you selling as a pet sitter? Peace of mind! Yes, you provide great pet care for busy owners, but that is the steak. The sizzle is how they will feel by using your services.

Now for the part where you get to toot your own horn for a minute. Once you have the attention of a potential client, it's time to show them why you are the best possible choice for them. This is where you let them know about any special experience or training you might have. You can tell them specifically what services you offer to make their lives easier. Show them that there is an element of commonality between you both. After all, you are both pet lovers for a start! Incorporating client testimonials and any noteworthy company achievements here will help lend credence to your abilities. You've already sold your services before hand. This is just assuring them that they made the right choice by deciding to use your company for all their pet care needs.

The hard part is now done, and you have your brilliantly written ad copy ready to go. Now what? What are the best ways to get your word out? As pet sitters, our target market covers a very small area. Unless you plan to drive more than work, you'll need to focus your advertising dollars across a very small geographical area.

There are several options for printed advertising. Newspapers, local magazines, neighborhood and local organization newsletters, direct mailings, and other print venues are some options for you to consider. There are all levels of pricing to think of with print ads. Do your research and find out what the odds of success are before you spend your money.

If you have the budget for it you can run a full page, half page, or quarter page ad with a photo in your local paper. This is a huge expense for the new business owner! You could run a small classified ad in your paper, or local sales sheet. The cost will be small; however, the return on investment might not make it worth it. You could do a little research on the newspaper you have in mind by looking through some of the ads listed and contacting a few of the companies running them. Often times business owners will be willing to share their experiences with you.

There are often local magazines or special interest magazines that you can consider advertising in. Advertising in magazines is usually a little costlier, and you also have to consider how broadly the magazine is distributed. Your advertising budget will go further if you make sure your ads are only distributed within your service area.

If you choose to advertise in neighborhood association newsletters, you will be able to target a very specific area for a reasonable cost. Special interest group newsletters that attract pet lovers are also a means of targeting your market, provided their distribution is within your area. There are many local breed fancier clubs and pet owner groups that you can contact regarding your advertising.

Another route to consider is direct mailings. Direct mailing costs to consider are the printing costs of the materials you plan to send out, the envelopes, and of course the postage as well. Also, mailing lists must be produced or purchased. You can make your own mailing lists by accessing the public records for your area via the courthouse for all pet license holders. It can be a time consuming and tedious task to sort through the information and distill it into the specific area of town you want to serve.

The return rate of direct mailing advertising is about 1%, statistically speaking. That means for every 100 pieces of mail you send out, you may get one customer. Consider the cost of 100 mailings against the benefit of one job. It could be well worth it, if you net a $200 or $300 pet sitting assignment as a result. You could reduce the cost of your mailings by using a postcard instead of a traditional marketing letter. You won't have as much space for your ad copy on a postcard, but with a little creativity you can still do the job!

Radio and television advertising is by far the most expensive way to go. Broadcasts will extend far beyond your area of service, so that you are not efficiently focusing on your target market using this medium. An exception to this is if you have a very large pet sitting company with sitters throughout your city. In that case, it could prove a good medium for your company.

Internet advertising is a very cost effective and results oriented medium for pet sitters. Your first and best ad, your website, is already up and running, right? There are pet sitter directories, pet sitting groups, pet sitting associations, and pet related websites with directories or linking services that you can use to promote your business. Local business directories and online yellow pages are also inexpensive options for advertising.

The internet provides 24 hour information access to anyone in need of just about anything. Directory searches can be conducted by zip code, so that your information is only displayed to people looking for service within your area. Sites like Yahoo Local and Google's Local Business Search are wonderful places to put your business information online.

Some directory listings allow for the insertion of your company information or ad copy. You can use your listing as you would use a print ad to sell your services. Other directories are formatted much like phone book listings with just the basic information visible. There are free and paid directories to consider. Those that are paid sites are very reasonably priced, and offer year long listings. Some offer additional helpful tools to make your pet sitting business run even more smoothly.

When considering which online sites you'd like to advertise with, it's wise to choose the ones that come up within the first page of a Google search. Most of your potential clients will click on links appearing at or near the top of the first page displayed when doing a search. You can type in "pet sitting services in (your area)" and see which listings come up first. Of course, listing your business on other sites, especially free ones, doesn't hurt either!

Tracking where your customers are hearing about you is an important step in organizing your marketing campaign. It will allow you to spend your advertising budget on those things that work for you, and let go of the things that don't. A good way to track your advertising effectiveness is to offer a specific discount code within each ad. You can use as many codes as necessary to narrow down your responses. For example, within your ad copy you can include the phrase "10% off first week of dog walking; just mention code xxxxx123." Customers will be happy to receive a discount, and you will be able to use this tracking information to your advantage.

Don't let your marketing campaign stagnate. Stay on top of your ads, ad copy, and public relations efforts. If you get complacent in your business building tasks, your bottom line will reflect it. Keep your website up to date, and keep your advertising copy fresh. If you add or delete services, make sure to change your marketing materials as well. Marketing is an ongoing process. Done correctly, it will keep the vitality in your business as well as your attitude toward your business.

> By far, the most successful advertising for us was internet directory listings. We listed our business on all of the free sites, and chose to pay for yearly listings on the top 3 sites appearing on Google when "pet sitters" was typed into the search box. This is where our customers all came from, aside from the referrals and word of mouth customers that came later from our existing client base. As we grew and developed a solid reputation we began to see more and more customer referrals.

Chapter Five

Interviewing for the Job
The "Meet & Greet"

Your phone is now ringing. Good job marketing your business; give yourself a big pat on the back! You are now well on your way to professional pet sitting. What happens next will no doubt cause you a bit of nerves, but fear not. You will make it through your first meet & greet and it will get easier with each one that you do.

After the first 50 job interviews, things began to flow very smoothly, but every once in a while someone will still throw me a curve! Being prepared for just about anything going into your meet & greets will keep you on your toes if something unexpected does come up.

Safety is always a concern when agreeing to meet a stranger in their home. I always let someone know where I'm going and how long I should be away. We have never had a bad experience in all the years we've been doing this, but it pays to be cautious! Listen to your gut feelings if something doesn't seem right. It's OK to cancel a meeting if things don't add up.

Be Prepared, Organized, and Professional

The best way to keep nerves at bay is to be prepared, organized, and professional. Having presentations that P.O.P. will project a positive image of you and your company. Clients will feel more at ease having you as their pet sitter. You will move smoothly and easily through your meetings regardless of whether it's your first or one hundred and first.

Preparation involves gathering as much information as possible beforehand. What types of pets will you be meeting? What are their names? Do they have any special needs? Ask questions when setting up your appointment, and jot down any notes that will help you once you arrive. Read and reread your contract and forms so that you know them very well. Map out your route to the clients home and print a copy of the directions if you are unfamiliar with the area. Pay special attention to the travel time involved and leave with plenty of time to get there. Do Not Be Late!

Organize your forms neatly in a folder. Add 2 business cards and your brochure if you have one. Make sure to have a pen with you. A clipboard will make it easier to take notes on pet care instructions and fill in any forms during your meeting.

Remain professional at all times. Remember, you are a business representative calling on a client. This is not a social visit. Dress appropriately, and act properly at all times. Pay attention to your posture when sitting or standing; don't slouch or slump back, no matter how comfortable the sofa is. Be respectful of your client and their home. Do not touch things or make yourself overly at home. The best rule of thumb is to behave as you would on any other job interview. After all, that's what this meeting really is.

> The first meet & greet that I did went pretty smoothly.
> I rang the doorbell with sweaty palms and butterflies,
> but fortunately the client was a very friendly "people

person" and we hit it off well. Having my forms arranged and organized helped to give me something to focus on other than my nervousness. Also, the dogs were very sweet and friendly, which helped a lot!

What to Expect

The initial consultation is what pet sitters commonly refer to as the "meet & greet." During this meeting you will get to know your client and their pet care needs. You will be gathering important information about the pet care routine unique to each client. The client will be able to show you around the home and tell you where to find everything you will need to get the job done. Most importantly, you will be able to interact with the pets that will be in your care.

Meeting new people can be exciting and fun. But for some, the prospect of interacting with strangers is uncomfortable at best. Keep this in mind when you meet with clients. They may be extremely happy to meet you, or they may feel a degree of discomfort during your consultation. Try to put them at ease as soon as possible. Your love of pets will give you common starting ground. You may also be somewhat uncomfortable meeting strangers. Do your best to project a positive, confident attitude. The more you interact with people, the easier it will become for you to do so comfortably.

Ask lots of questions about the pets, their routines, schedules and needs. Take notes. Listen carefully to the client. Don't be afraid to ask for clarification if you are unsure about anything. Your goal is to keep the pets routine as intact as possible. Consistency will help pets to be comfortable while their owners are away. Favorite activities, games, routes for walks, and even music or television stations are worth noting.

Use your forms to document information and keep it on file for future sits. You can go over the forms line by line and fill them in with the client, or leave the forms for clients to fill in at their convenience. If you choose to fill the forms in during your meeting, it will take more time. If you leave the forms with the client, you run the risk of finding incomplete or blank forms when you return to do the sit. Decide what will work best for each individual client and proceed accordingly.
Ask to be shown where all pet care items are kept. You will also want to know about any cleaning supplies, in the event of any pet "accidents" as well. Again, take notes. Refer to your notes for future bookings and remember to ask if anything has changed since your last visit.

The most important part of the meet & greet is to get to know the pets you'll be caring for. Some pets will be timid and shy, and some won't be able to get enough of you! Pay special attention to any aggressive behavior. You will have to make a decision quickly if the pet seems too aggressive to handle. Very few pets will fall under this category, but you don't want to be faced with an animal that you can't care for after the owners are away.

Allow pets to come to you. Don't rush them into interacting with you. If they seem shy, try sitting on the floor if possible and just pretend not to notice them. Often, curiosity will get the best of them and they will come over to see what you are all about. Having treats on hand helps, but make sure to get owners permission first. Pets will take their queue from their owners, and consider it OK for you to be in their homes if they see it is OK with the client.

Meeting the pets now will make caring for them later easier. They will remember you and the positive interaction they had when you first met. They will especially remember any treats or goodies. This can work to your advantage in most cases, but beware of the goodie- stealing dog that knows just which pocket the treats are in. You may find yourself with a hole in your clothes and possibly worse.

Each meet & greet has been an adventure. The personalities that I've come in contact with have been quite varied. I was very lucky in my last "outside job" to have been given a good deal of communication training. Being aware of the different personality types and communication styles helps to talk to people the way they want to be spoken to. The golden rule is to do unto others as you would have them do unto you, but the platinum rule is to do unto others as *they* would have you do unto *them*!

Collecting all Pertinent Information

Since you have either designed or purchased forms to help collect the information you need, this part will be a snap. You will want to know a number of things about the pets and their daily routines.

Some important things to know are:
- Names, ages, and health conditions of pets
- Name of veterinarian or clinic they visit

- Emergency contact names and numbers
- Feeding schedule and amount
- Favorite games, toys, treats, etc.
- Areas where the pets are and are not allowed
- Any commands used
- Information about the house alarms, lights, parking, mail service, etc
- Location of all pet care items
- Location of cleaning supplies and trash cans

In addition to this information you will need to have clients sign a contract which outlines your rates, when payment is expected, what you will be responsible for, and any additional items you agree on. Should any problems arise later, like late payment or questions on liability, this contract will be very important.

Keep all forms, contracts, and notes safe in a file cabinet or other container. You can create your own file system if you like, as long as you can quickly find any client information you need.

> Keeping my presentations no longer than 15 minutes helps to move things along and allows customers time to ask questions and let me know what they need. I usually arrange my forms in a certain order and go over them with the client, but allow the customers to complete them at their leisure before the sit begins.

Finally, you will want to make arrangements for entry into the home. Most clients will prefer to give you a key, but some will provide garage codes or openers, or other means of access. You can offer a key storage service in which you keep clients keys on file for future use, or make an appointment to return the key after the sit is complete.

Test the key before leaving your meet & greet. If the client provided you with other means of entry, test that as well. You don't want to be unable to get inside to care for pets when the owners are somewhere in the Bahamas! Never put identifying information on keys or remotes. Use a code system and temporary tag to keep keys organized. If you store them, invest in a small key safe that can be locked and stored securely. These extra measures will provide reassurance to security conscious clients.

Most of our customers prefer to keep a key on file for future sits. We have a key safe with over 120 keys in it, which are all marked with codes to protect our clients' property should they fall into the wrong hands. When we have a sit come up all we have to do is go to the client file and determine the code based on information on the file, which only we know about.

If a customer wishes to have their key returned, we charge a key drop off fee to cover our time and gas. If we need to pick up a key we do the same. Some key drops and pick ups are inconvenient, as the clients are only available at a certain time when we are not usually in the area, or after regular business hours.

We have never had a key fail to work, but we did have a doorknob fall off once. The knob was not in the best shape when we tested the key, but I didn't think much of it until our third visit, when it fell of into my hand! Fortunately, my husband was there and managed to put it back together while I went in and took care of the pets. Good thing too, as the owners were away in Africa at the time. We would have had to get a locksmith to come out and repair the door; and we would have had to cover the expense until we were able to bill the client at the end of the sit. Now I always check doorknobs and ask clients what arrangements they have made in the event that something goes wrong with anything in the house.

Chapter Six

Great! You're Hired. Now What?
Preparing for the Job

Congratulations! You're hired. Now it's time to get prepared to do the job. If you've filled out the forms during your meet & greet, now is a good time to go over them. Are there any specific times that the client requests visits? Do the pets have any special needs that you are aware of? Refer to your notes and make a plan of action for each sit. If you have left the forms for the clients to complete later, your notes will help give you an idea of what you'll need to do.

You can prepare yourself by making sure you have everything that you will need for the job. Bring along a pen or two, your sit log sheets, and most importantly, the key. A helpful tool you can take with you for pet sitting is a small "sit kit," which you can keep in the trunk of your car. You can use a small plastic tub with a lid to keep everything organized. Items to include in this kit are:
- A flashlight (WITH fresh batteries)
- Paper towels
- A roll of garbage bags
- Hand sanitizer
- A first aid kit
- Mosquito repellent

When I first started sitting, I kept a huge assortment of stuff in my trunk. I had everything imaginable in there —gloves, dustpan, small shovel, carpet cleaner, yard tools, pet shampoo, a blow drier, towels, you name it!

After driving around with about 10 lbs. of extra weight for some months, I realized that there were only a couple of things that I actually had ever used. I lightened the load and never missed any of it.

You will have a pretty good idea what you'll need to do each visit based on your initial consultation. Some of the things you'll probably be doing include feeding and watering pets, bringing in mail and newspapers, adjusting blinds and lights, watering houseplants, scooping litter boxes, and of course giving love and attention to the pets. You may be asked to do other simple tasks around the home, such as turning sprinklers on and off, or turning televisions or radios on for the pets.

The strangest request that was ever made of me was to "feed" a sour dough starter. This involved adding flour after removing some of the contents of a jar every couple of days. It was kind of like a kitchen science experiment!

Be careful to follow the feeding instructions given to you very carefully. Don't add an extra scoop or two of kibble to the bowl because it doesn't look like enough, or alter the pet's diet in any way. Also, change water bowls each visit to keep drinking water fresh. You may need to wash the food and water bowls according to instructions.

Place the mail and newspapers neatly in the agreed upon spot. Keep everything well organized and presentable. You never know when a client may come home early, and you want everything to be in order at all times. Don't be tempted to let things go till the final visit.

Rotating lighting and opening or closing blinds periodically helps to give the home an occupied look should anyone be watching the house. Simple measures offer added security while owners are away and the house sits empty.

If you are asked to water plants, watch out for leaky containers. An ounce of prevention can save you a pound of clean up time! If possible, move the plants to a safe area, such as a sink. For larger floor plants that can't be moved, give them a very small drink first to make sure it's safe. When watering plants it's best to err on the side of less water. They will make a full and quick recovery from under watering, but if you over-water, it could mean the end of them.

Sweep up any pet hair or food messes each visit. Keep the home nice and clean. If you are sitting for cats, watch out for litter tracked around the litter box. Cat litter can scratch floors if stepped on just right. It's also a good idea to vacuum any pet hair from the carpet every few days, if the pets are OK with this. If they are very nervous then you may want to skip this step. Keep the home looking like you want it to look when your client gets home. That way you won't be caught unawares if they do return early.

We've had clients return home early on many occasions. I never worry much about it, because everything is left in order each visit. I have heard stories from clients about former sitters leaving things a mess. When the clients came home they were very unhappy and quit using that company. I'm sure the sitters planned to sweep and tidy up on their last visit, but unfortunately they didn't get the chance.

Knowing what each pet requires will make the pet care routine easy. If pets have any special needs, follow the owner's instructions to the letter. Some animals will need a bit of time to warm up to you. After a few visits they will usually be very happy to see you. If they are fearful or uncomfortable, you can try putting them at ease by sitting on the floor and offering treats (if allowed). Try not to force the issue if they are very shy.

If you do happen to sit for a very shy dog, leashing up for a trip outside may be a challenge. If there is no back yard available for the dogs to relieve themselves in, you may find yourself in a jam. Most pets will submit to being leashed without incident. Be patient, and if you can't do it, just try again a little later.

If you find yourself in a situation where something goes wrong, contact your client or the emergency contact listed on your form immediately. If you are unable to get in touch with someone, you may be forced to use your best judgment to deal with the problem at hand. Some things that could go wrong include:
- Sick Pets
- Plumbing Problems
- Burglary or Break-in
- Structural Problem with the House
- Emergency Weather Situation
- Fire, Flood, or Other Disaster
- Emergency Evacuation of the Area

A Disaster Preparedness Plan is very important. You should discuss these possibilities with your clients and make sure you are both in agreement as to the course of action to be taken in the event of an incident. This is especially imperative if you live in an area where weather can be an issue, or wild fires are prone to occur.

One of the worst experiences we had during our first year was in sitting for an elderly dog. The owners mentioned in passing that she had developed a case of stress related diarrhea once while in the care of a neighbor. She didn't seem too concerned about it during our meet & greet. I didn't question her further due to her nonchalant attitude. That was mistake number one.

When we arrived to do the first sit, there was a bit of mess waiting for us. It was on a tiled area and fairly easy to clean. I didn't think any more of it until we arrived for the second visit.

It was Christmastime, and there was a tree with presents in the living room. This was to prove a very bad thing! There was dog poo from one room to the other, and even on the coffee table and Christmas presents. Although we did our best to clean things up, the owners had only left a few paper towels and a nearly empty bottle of carpet cleaner.

Our biggest mistake was in trying to deal with the problem. I should have called the client right away at the first sign of trouble and let her decide how to proceed. Instead we spent way too much time trying to fix things, and ended up buying cleaning supplies to boot.

In the end, she hired a professional carpet cleaner to come out and clean the mess up before they returned home. Guess who had to let the workmen in and stick around while they did their job. I didn't charge for the extra time I spent (although-- mistake number three-- I should have!) because I felt guilty for not contacting the client right away.

The worst part was that she was totally rude afterwards, and didn't even acknowledge that we went out of our way to accommodate her and make things right. She never called us again, and we were just fine with that!

After that incident, we always stressed the need for adequate cleaning supplies, and called the client right away if anything was just the least bit out of order.

Chapter 7

Keeping Track
Record Keeping, Billing, and Administrative Duties

Now that you're up and running, you'll need to develop a method for keeping your business records straight. If you set up a good system to tackle all of the accounting, record keeping, and other "admin" tasks, and stay on top of the job, you'll find it is really not that hard. Even if you have never had any office experience you can manage quite well. The secret is to stay organized and set aside a certain amount of time each week for office duty.

As a business owner you will need to wear many hats. You will become a jack of all trades, so to speak. The good news is that you can decide what works best for you, and you can change most procedures if you find they no longer do work. The one exception to this is the accounting method you plan to use. Once you commit to an accounting method, you're pretty much obligated to continue using it for I.R.S. purposes.

Accounting

There are two methods of accounting. One is the cash method. In this method, you account only for what has been paid to you. Outstanding invoices are not included in your income figures until you receive payment.

The accrual method is another option. Using this accounting procedure, all income is declared, including any unpaid balances owed to you. These outstanding invoices are counted as income as soon as you send them out. Using the accrual method of accounting will often result in making your business look like it currently has more money than it actually does. This can work against you at tax time.

The advice of a certified public accountant or tax professional can help you decide which method is right for you. Your C.P.A. can help you to get the most out of your business deductions, and can be a valuable asset during tax time. If you choose to do your own accounting and bookkeeping, the I.R.S. offers lots of information to help you. Take the time to study this material, and invest in a good basic business accounting book.

Spreadsheets are very helpful for keeping track of your business expenditures. You can find templates online that can be customized to fit your needs. Track all income and expenses weekly, and total them monthly using your spreadsheet. Mileage can also be documented on your spreadsheet for tax deduction purposes. If you prefer to use pencil and paper, you can purchase ledger paper at the office supply store. Use this just as you would a computer spreadsheet.

Keep all receipts for business related purchases, arrange them by month and file them. You will need to take these to your accountant if you use one. If you do your own bookkeeping, use them to verify information on your ledger. Should you ever face a tax audit, you will definitely need all receipts for expenses claimed as business deductions.

You will also need to keep a record of your mileage. If you have a vehicle used strictly for business travel, you will have an easier time keeping track of your deductible miles. If you do use your vehicle for both personal and business travel, you will need to be careful to only deduct the miles driven for business purposes. A simple mileage log is needed, and you will be glad to have it in case of an I.R.S. audit. Be sure to write your beginning and ending mileage in your log book every day.

Keeping meticulous records will help you to know exactly how your business is doing financially. It will also make tax preparation much easier. If you need to prove income for any reason, such as to seek bank loans, having your records in order will relieve much of the stress associated with the transaction.   It is also much easier to keep up with your bookkeeping as you go rather than trying to put it all in order on the last day of the tax season.

Record Keeping

As a pet sitter, you will be privy to quite a bit of sensitive information, such as alarm codes, home access codes, and other important information about your clients. Always be discreet, and keep files safely stored. Coding keys and protecting your files may seem unnecessary, but if your office or car is ever burglarized, you can at least feel confident that your client's property is secure. Keeping everything safe can help prevent claims against your pet sitting insurance as well, keeping your premiums from going up unexpectedly.

If you have the space, consider investing in a locking file cabinet. You can set up your client files in whatever way works best for you. Things to keep in the file folders include client forms, notes, any correspondence between the client and yourself, and copies of past invoices.

Keeping your folders arranged alphabetically by clients' last names will help you be able find needed files quickly and easily. When you book a sit, you can pull the client file and confirm that there have been no changes since your last visit. If anything has changed, make notes and place it in the folder.

Periodically update your files to keep everything current. If you have inactive accounts, or clients that have moved away, you can store these files in a separate area to make room for new client files. Keep all contact phone numbers up to date, and be sure to maintain correct addresses for your client base. If you have a computerized customer database, make the appropriate changes there also. Contacting your clients from time to time to verify information serves to keep you in their minds as well. You will achieve two things at once.

Billing

Billing your clients is fairly easy and painless. Keeping track of what is owed to you can be a little more challenging. You can eliminate much of the work by billing in advance. Otherwise, you will need to set up a method to keep you aware of what is owed to you and by whom. Billing in advance has many advantages over invoicing after the work is done, however it is easier to make changes to the amounts due if you do bill upon completion of the sits. If a customer adds visits, you can simply apply the additional charges to the invoice due.

One simple way to stay on top of your invoices is to keep two separate files. One file should be marked "Invoices Due," and one should say "Invoices Paid." A rubber stamp marked "Paid" can be helpful as well. When payments arrive in the mail or you collect them in person, stamp the invoices on file as paid and put them in the correct folder as you prepare your bank deposit. Make it a habit to do this every time you receive payments. If you let the paid invoices go unmarked too long, you may forget that you were indeed compensated for your work.

Sometimes, payments are slow to arrive, or do not arrive at all. You will be forced to make an uncomfortable telephone call to remind late paying customers that their invoices are overdue. Letters are a good way to have written record of demand for payment. Keep in mind that you will need a plan should you be forced to take further action. As a last resort, you may need to consider filing suit in small claims court to collect your payment.

Non-paying customers are the exception and certainly not the norm, but it does happen. Keep a straight head and do not take it personally. You may not be able to salvage the business relationship, but always remember your business reputation. Never treat a client rudely or harass them, regardless of how frustrated you may feel.

> We always bill our daily dog walking customers 2 weeks in advance. This makes it easier to keep track of. Everyone has a due date of the 1st and 15th of each month.

In the past, we billed after each two week cycle, but unfortunately had one non-paying and several late paying customers that forced us to change our policies.

We do still bill our pet sitting customers after the sits are complete. There have been a few slow payers, but we have never had anyone refuse to pay their bill.

Administrative Duties

Miscellaneous duties involved in running your business include sending and answering e-mails and correspondence, answering and returning telephone calls, database setup and maintenance, ongoing market research, copying and filing business forms, website maintenance, keeping marketing materials stocked and ready to use, tracking your advertising and marketing results, and many more "behind the scenes" tasks that keep your business going. Once you get a system in place, these responsibilities aren't nearly as bad as they may sound. You can set aside a few hours a week to get most of your office work done.

If it all sounds overwhelming to you, consider hiring a part time helper, or outsourcing the administrative tasks to a virtual assistant. You may even be able to barter your pet sitting services in exchange for administrative help. The important thing to remember is not to let your office work pile up on you. Tackle small tasks well before they get out of hand.

I chose to do all of our accounting, administrative duties and bookkeeping myself. This was again due to my need to be fully involved in all aspects of running our business. It has been fairly easy to keep track of everything using Microsoft Excel.

There are some great business accounting programs out there, but the method I developed is more of a hybrid pen and paper/ computerized style of bookkeeping.

I use spreadsheets to document everything, but print them out, attach receipts and bank statements, and file them away for tax time. I like having the hard copies handy to refer to when doing my calculations. I guess this means that I'm not quite as computer dependent as I like to think I am!

I have to be honest. There are many things I would rather be doing than working on the administrative side of the business. It was a real challenge to write this chapter. Just thinking of doing office work makes me want to go outside and play with my canine friends!

Chapter 8

Ready, Set, Grow!
Hiring to Meet Business Demands

As your pet sitting business becomes more successful, you will develop a following of loyal customers. You will also receive referrals from them. Combine this with your ongoing advertising, marketing, and p.r. efforts and you may find yourself with more business than you can handle single-handedly.

You will have to make a decision when you reach this point. You can either turn customers away, find someone to assist you, or refer clients to other sitters you may know. If you do decide to refuse work, you run the risk of alienating your clients. A logical step then becomes to hire outside help.

Employee vs. Independent Contractor

You can choose to hire an employee or an independent contractor to fill your needs. Of course, as in all things, there are pro's and con's to each type of worker.

According to the I.R. S. website, www.irs.gov, the definition of an employee is as follows:

"Under common-law rules, anyone who performs services for you is your employee *if you can control what will be done and how it will be done.* This is so even when you give the employee freedom of action. What matters is that you have the right to control the details of how the services are performed."

If you do choose to hire an employee, you will have more control over the way in which they perform the job. However, as an employer, you will become responsible for a number of things. You must withhold income taxes and FICA from your employee's pay. In addition, you will be responsible for paying the employer share of FICA. You must also pay federal unemployment (FUTA) tax of 6.2% before any state credits on wages up to $7,000 annually. Depending on your state and county, there may be additional requirements of you as an employer.

If this sounds like more than you'd prefer to be responsible for, you can consider hiring an independent contractor. Again, according to the I.R.S website, the guideline that determines independent contractor status is:

"The general rule is that an individual is an independent contractor if you, the person for whom the services are performed, have the *right to control or direct only the result of the work and not the means and methods of accomplishing the result.*"

What this means is that you will have very little say in the manner in which the work will be performed. Company standards and practices do not apply to independent contractors, and you cannot specify anything other than the end result of their efforts, i.e. the pets receive visits.

Independent contractors are themselves business owners, and as such are solely responsible for paying income taxes and insuring that their FICA is covered. Therefore, you will not have to worry about withholdings or deductions for anyone working for you as an independent contractor.

The line between employee and i.c. can become blurred in many instances. Take great care to adhere to the standards outlined by the I.R.S.; if you fail to do so, there could be severe tax penalties involved. The best way to make sure that you are in the clear is to consult them directly. The website also provides helpful information.

Finding the Right Person for the Job

If you do decide to take on the responsibility of an employee, you'll need to find a good fit for your company. Hiring a total stranger to such a position of trust can be a nerve-racking notion. After all, you have worked hard to foster your customer relationships. It is your business reputation on the line should anything go wrong.

The best steps to hiring wisely are to screen carefully, and seek out the best candidate for the job through interview questions, references, and possibly even background checks.

Consider the best places to find prospective employees. A very good way to find help is usually by referral. Knowing someone who can vouch for the character of the applicant can be helpful. Don't be afraid to turn down individuals that don't meet your standards. This is your business, and your reputation!

Another way to find candidates is to advertise the position in your local newspaper. This isn't always the best way to go. You will be casting your net over a huge sea of people in hopes of finding one gem. If you have the time and patience to review applications, interview potential sitters, and check multiple references, then great. But since you're looking for help, it's a good bet that you do not have that kind of free time.

An alternative is to advertise to a small group of people that represent more of the qualities you are hoping to find in your applicants. Groups involved in pet rescue, pet care, and general animal interest may present a better pool to choose from than the general public.

The Interview Process

Once you have a few applications, it's time to start the interview process. You'll want to meet with prospective employees and get an idea of what they are all about. Ask lots of open-ended questions to allow them to share their pet care, customer service, and business views with you.

Notice body language and non-verbal communication as well as verbal statements. Also take note of neatness and personal hygiene. Ask yourself if you would feel comfortable having each applicant alone in your home. Do they project an image of trustworthiness?

Once you have narrowed your search down to one or two applicants, it's time to check references. You'll want to contact former employers and business references to make sure potential employees are honest and have good work ethics. Again, listen carefully to intent as well as verbiage.

Some additional considerations in hiring an employee are:

- Training
- Obtaining pet sitting insurance for your employee(s)
- Obtaining a signed non-compete contract
- Routing and scheduling your staff
- Payroll accounting and pay distribution
- Background check
- Surety bonding

If you decide that an independent contractor is the best solution for you, you will want to conduct an interview and check references as well. Remember that independent contractors are also pet sitting business owners like you. Try to contract with a pet sitter that holds similar views on pet care and customer service to your own. Also make sure that your contractor carries the appropriate pet sitting insurance.

Since independent contractors handle all of their own accounting and taxes, you will pay them the agreed upon amount without deducting anything. You will, however, need to keep track of how much you pay your i.c.'s and file appropriate forms with the I.R.S. (and possibly your state) annually.

Finally, if you prefer to refer work out to fellow pet sitters, make sure you network with them and know their standards and practices. Many sitters form loose networking groups and pass work to each other when the workload becomes too much for them. Some pet sitters arrange referral fees between each other in the form of a set dollar amount or percentage of the total sit fee.

Although I have been responsible for hiring, training, and managing a team of employees in the past, I have never hired an employee or i.c. for Spot Check. I have referred work out to other sitters in the area on many occasions.

The sitters in my area are a great bunch of people over-all, and I am glad to send them work from time to time. The ethics and standards of professionals with whom I network are very high, so I feel comfortable that they will do a great job for the customer.

It's been nice getting to know other area sitters. There is a real sense of camaraderie within the group, and no competitiveness or animosity at all. We are all partners in arms, so to speak, and there is more than enough work to go around.

Chapter 9

Keep Your Customers Happy!
Ace Customer Service

Who are your most valuable customers? Your current customers are! The costs involved in finding new customers are far greater than the costs of maintaining existing customers. Keep them happy and give them more than they expect and you will hold on to them. Treat them well and develop good business relationships with each of them.

Ace customer service involves treating your customers the way *they* want to be treated. Listen to their needs and respond quickly. If your customer has a concern, address it immediately. When a problem arises, it is an opportunity for you. Use it wisely and give your clients stellar treatment. They will remember how you treated them long after they have forgotten what the problem was.

Think about a great customer service experience you had in the past. Remember how good you felt? Give your customers that same good feeling every chance you get! Good customer service is very simple. It involves listening, offering solutions, and following through, and being proactive. That's it. Do these 4 things and you will keep your clients happy.

Listening

Listen to your customers concerns. If a client comes to you with a complaint, consider it a great compliment. Most customers will not complain unless they value the business relationship. The more usual reaction is to simply find another service provider to do business with. Keep this in mind when you listen to complaints and it will make it much easier to stay positive and avoid taking things personally.

Allow clients to tell you what's on their mind. It's hard to sit quietly and just focus on what people are saying to you sometimes, but it is imperative if you want to provide top notch service. Do not think about how you will respond. Just listen. Try to discover the facts *as your customer sees them*. Let them arrive at their point in their own words. Do not interrupt. Some times customers really need to vent their frustrations more than anything else. Let them blow off this steam and they will be much easier to deal with afterwards.

Once they have stated their problem or concern, confirm that you have understood by paraphrasing. You can say, "Just to make sure I understand, you feel that ...." If they correct you, restate the problem again until you both feel that the subject is clear. It is important to be sure of what the problem is before you can move on to the next step.

Offering Solutions

Once you have listened carefully to your client, and have made certain that you understand the concern, it's time to offer solutions. You can ask directly what your client would like to see happen. If you do take this direct route, be cautious to phrase your question carefully. You can offer two or more possible solutions and let your client decide which solution will work best for them. You can also offer one solution that you feel comfortable will work best.

Only offer solutions that are in your power to provide. Don't rely on third parties to come through for you. And always under-promise and over-deliver! If you make promises that you will have a hard time keeping, you risk angering your customer further and possibly losing their business. It is much better to promise less than you know you are able to do, and then do more.

Following Through

Always follow through! After arriving at an acceptable solution, make it happen immediately. Be sure that you contact your customer once you have done what was promised to insure that everything is to their liking. Don't miss this opportunity to ask questions. If for some reason the response indicates less than 100% satisfaction, go back to step one and start again.

There will always be those people whom you can never fully please, but they are very rare. Customers who have gone to the trouble of contacting you are usually looking for a reasonable resolution. By providing quick response, and showing that you value them as your client, you send the message that they are very important to you and your business.

If you consistently provide great customer service, you will develop a reputation for being a great service provider. Your clients will share their positive experiences with people they know. Statistically, customers will share bad experiences with 3 other people, but only tell only 1 person of a good one. It's in every business owner's best interest to turn all potentially bad experiences into excellent ones!

Being Proactive

Another aspect of great customer service is to be proactive, and go the extra mile every day. If you offer value added services that your competition is not offering for the same price as standard service, customers will recognize that. They will become loyal clients, and tell others as well.

There are many ways to show your customers how much they mean to you. If you have pets' birth dates on file, you can send a birthday card or drop off a treat with a nice note attached. If you come across information that your clients may find useful, such as a breed-specific article, you might want to clip it and send it with a short note. This not only lets them know that you are thinking of them and their pets, but also keeps you fresh in their minds, should someone ask them about pet sitters.

Opinion surveys are also a great tool to find out what each client thinks about your service. Leave a survey at the end of each sit, or periodically leave one for your daily dog walks. Be sure to thank your customers for taking the time to complete the surveys. A small discount coupon good toward future services is also a thoughtful way to say thanks, and will be appreciated.

If you haven't heard from a client in a while, you can send a postcard letting them know that you are thinking of them and their pets. Be sure to hand write a short note, and always mention the pets by name. Giving it a personal touch will make it more sincere than just sending out a generic form letter style card.

You can be creative in coming up with ways to set yourself apart from the pack in the eyes of your customers. The most important thing is to make a genuine effort to always show your clients how much you appreciate their choice to do business with you. After all, there are many pet sitters out there and many more kids down the street ready to offer pet care. When pet owners choose you, they are entrusting not only their homes and possessions to you, but their beloved furry family members as well.

The first time I had an unhappy customer that could not be soothed, I was taken completely aback. I had done everything right, plus gone above and beyond in accommodating this client. It was a learning experience for me to say the least. The most valuable lesson that I took away from this encounter is that each of us has a different perspective when looking at an identical situation.

What I saw as good service, and what most other customers saw as such was not necessarily perceived that way by this individual. After much listening and solution offering, it became apparent that we could not arrive at a suitable resolution. Unfortunately there was no option other than to end our business relationship.

Customers like this come along very rarely. We have otherwise never had a problem that couldn't be solved by following the steps outlined in this chapter. The focus for Spot Check is to develop strong working relationships with our customers and nurture these relationships on an ongoing basis. If we ever do make a mistake, it is much easier for clients to forgive us and allow us to make it up to them.

Chapter Ten

Putting It All Together and Making It Work for You
Conclusion

In the previous eight chapters, we've talked about many aspects of starting and running a professional pet sitting business. We have covered the realities of pet sitting, business structures, licensing, banking, insurance, communications, advertising, marketing, public relations, meeting clients, what to do on the job, administrative and bookkeeping duties, hiring, and customer service.

Of course, it's impossible to cover, or even remember absolutely everything. However, you should now have a very good understanding of the pet sitting business. This will allow you to form your own ideas and plans that will work best for you. Hopefully you will go into your new business venture with your eyes wide open and with a broad array of tools to help you get going.

But, the only way to really figure out what will best suit your needs is to get out there and get the experience first hand. Don't be afraid to learn as you go. Keep educating yourself on pet care and on business practices as well. As long as you have a strong knowledge of pets and how to care for them, the rest will be easy to learn.

There are many friendly and helpful pet sitters out there who are glad to share their expertise with you. You can seek them out online in pet sitting forums, or look to local sitters who might be interested in forming networking groups or referral systems.

In closing, here are a few useful things I have learned during my years of caring for pets:

- NEVER play fetch with a large dog on a retractable leash.
- Giving a cat a pill can be tricky; giving a snake a shot requires extra limbs and nerves of steel.
- Male dogs will relieve themselves on just about anything with vertical height. Avoid freshly detailed car tires, trash cans, recycling bins, and baby carriages. Also, they have remarkable bladder capacities, so never underestimate their ability to "produce."
- Boxers can fling drool about 6 to 8 feet, more on warm days.
- Boxer drool is very difficult to wipe from sunglasses.
- Bunnies have very large teeth. No matter how cute they are, avoid kissing them on their noses.
- Do not hold hermit crabs in the palm of your hand. Ever.
- Always avoid standing too close to an excited Yorkie while wearing flip-flops.
- The term *Love*birds is very misleading. Lovebirds have very sharp beaks and surprisingly large attitudes for such small creatures.
- Not all dogs named "Killer" are mean.
- Not all cats named "Lovey" are nice.

- Declawed cats retain the ability to make you bleed.
- Despite the old adage, music does *not* necessarily tame the savage beast. Especially heavy metal and punk rock.
- Ferrets can fit through an opening roughly the size of a half dollar, sometimes smaller, if the ferret is especially motivated.
- Driving faster in order to reduce the overall travel time does not help car-sick cats and dogs hold onto their stomach contents.
- Always check plastic grocery bags for holes very carefully before using them to pick up dog waste or clean litter boxes.
- If the combined weight of the dogs you're walking is greater than your own, you might want to consider walking them one at a time.
- Skinned knees take about a week to heal; dislocated shoulders require considerably longer.
- Turtles are a lot faster than they'd like you to think they are.
- Turtles also have very sharp beaks, and some are not afraid to use them.
- Never grab an iguana by the tail.
- It takes nearly a year for an iguana to regrow its tail.
- Some dogs will swallow just about anything.
- It can take over a week for that just about anything to make its way through a dog's digestive tract.
- Keep a tight grip on leashes. Even the elderly, docile dog that has walked beside you at heel for the last 3 years has the potential to make you chase him for hours.

Part II

Resources

In part two, you will find a ton of useful resources to help you along even further. Use the information provided to get a jump start in your new career. The content was collected not only over the course of years in the pet sitting business, but many prior years in the general business sector.

Communication

Personality Types & Communication Styles

There are 4 basic personality types. Although we all possess some characteristics of each style, there is one dominant type that is prevalent in everyone. Learning to recognize and work with different personality types will be of tremendous benefit to you in both your business and personal relationships.

The Driver

The Driver personality is also called The Director. Drivers are task oriented rather than people oriented individuals. They can often be seen as rude or harsh, although they do not intend to be. They often work in positions of power. Drivers are usually focused on results and efficiency.

Drivers are more likely to be poor listeners, and seem inflexible. They speak in a forceful tone, at a fast pace. They state more than they ask, talk more than listen, make strong statements, and are quick to anger.

Physical signs of a Driver include a firm handshake, steady eye contact, fast paced behavior, and a very self confident and decisive attitude.

How to Communicate with Drivers

Keep things concise and to the point. Be formal, clear, specific, brief, and efficient. Come prepared with all requirements, objectives and support materials in a well organized package. Present your facts logically. Ask specific questions. Provide alternatives for making their own decisions. Provide facts and figures about the probability of success and effectiveness of options. If you disagree, take issue with the facts, not the person. After talking business, depart graciously.

The Expressive

Expressives are also called The Socializer. Many Expressives excel in the field of sales. They are optimistic, enthusiastic, creative, and possess strong creative skills. They put relationships before results, and therefore are easily loved.

People who fall into this category are spontaneous, reactive, impulsive, intuitive, and sometimes dramatic. They have short attention spans and persuasive personalities.

Expressive individuals can be recognized by such physical traits as animated facial expressions, big gestures, contact oriented, and they tend to create disorganized piles.

Communicating with Expressives

Plan interaction that supports their dreams and intuitions. Allow time for relating and socializing. Talk about people and their ideas. Focus on people and action items. Don't deal with extensive details—put them in writing. Ask for their opinions, don't be impersonal. Provide ideas and testimonials. Continue supporting the relationship. Be casual.

Amiables

Amiables, also known as The Supporters, are very sensitive people that tend to be most focused on the needs of others. They are respectful, willing, and agreeable. They do not like risks. Amiables function well in support roles in the business environment.

These personality types are not assertive. They are responsive to others, They are not goal oriented, as a general rule. Sometimes their soft-heartedness leads to oversensitivity.

Some visual queues to help recognize amiables include intermittent eye contact, gentle handshakes, patience, and slower moving body language.

Communicating with Amiables

Start with a social interaction; break the ice, and use time to be agreeable. Show sincere interest in them as people and find areas of common ground. Be candid and open. Patiently draw out personal ideas. Listen and be responsive. Present your case smoothly, non-threateningly. Ask specific "how?" questions to elicit their opinions. If you disagree, look for hurt feelings. Move in an informal but orderly way. Provide personal assurances and guarantees. If decision is required, give them time to think.

Analyticals

Analytical individuals are also called The Clinician. They are neither assertive nor responsive. They are very precise and business-like. Analyticals tend to be rational and motivated by logic. You might find them working in fields such as accounting or science.

Although rational and cooperative, Analyticals distrust those with persuasive personalities. They are very security conscious, self controlled and serious. This type of person prefers to have things in writing. They can often be critical, aloof, and skeptical.

Physical signs of this personality style include few facial expressions, non-contact oriented, little or no gestures, slower moving, and written communication preferences.

Communicating with Analyticals

Prepare your presentation in advance. Be accurate and formal. Approach them in a straight-forward, but direct way. Stick to business. Support their logical and methodical approach; build your credibility by listing pros and cons to any suggestion you may make. Make an organized contribution to their efforts. Present specifics and do what you say you will do. Draw up a plan of action with scheduled dates and milestones. Be conservative. If you disagree, prove it with facts and data or testimonials. Provide them with the information and the time to make a decision.

Listening

Listening is a vital part of the communication process. We spend approximately 60% of our time listening, but unfortunately most of us do not do it very well.

Most people speak at a rate of 125 to 150 words per minute, while the human brain is easily able to process between 400 and 600 words per minute. What do you do with all of the time in between? Have you ever noticed yourself trying to think of a response to what someone is saying before they have ever even finished their sentence? If you are like most people, the answer is probably yes. Unfortunately, we run the risk of miscommunication when we do this. Practice focusing on what the other person is saying, rather than thinking ahead. Active listening is a learned skill and requires practice and patience.

One of the most effective tools you can use in communication is the use of silence. Give the other person your full attention and process the information before you respond. This would be a good time to paraphrase information to make sure that you are "on the same page."

Empathy is the ability to look at the situation from the other person's viewpoint, and put yourself in that persons position in order to really try to understand how that person feels. Understanding another person's feelings does not mean that you are forced to agree with or accept that viewpoint. It merely means that you are trying to experience the situation as if you were the other person. Such understanding is the basis of effective communication. Flexibility in dealing with those needs increases your ability to communicate effectively.

When listening for the total message, not only listen to the content of the message, but the intent as well. Look for body language, tone of voice, and facial expressions. Try to avoid selective listening—hearing only what you wish to hear. Listen with an open mind, and resist the temptation to interrupt or overreact. Maintain positive body language and eye contact so that others know you are interested in what they have to say.

Some key actions involved in listening effectively:

- Do not interrupt
- Listen for intent as well as content
- Demonstrate empathy
- Show that you are listening
- Ask questions
- Paraphrase
- Minimize distractions

Comparative Charts

Web Hosting Comparison Chart

Host	Price/ month	Dom- ain Price	Disk Space	FTP	E- Comm- erce tools	Email Accounts
Just host	3.95	Free	Unlimited	Yes	Yes	Unlimited
Fat Cow	4.66	Free	Unlimited	Yes	Yes	Unlimited
Bluehost	6.95	Free	Unlimited	Yes	Yes	2500
Yahoo	6.47	Free	Unlimited	Yes	Limit- ed	1000
Hostmonster	4.95	Free	Unlimited	Yes	Yes	Unlimited
Inmotion	6.95	Free	Unlimited	No	Limit- ed	5000
Supergreen	5.95	Free	Unlimited	Yes	Yes	Unlimited
Greengeeks	7.95	Free	Unlimited	Yes	Yes	Unlimited
Fastdomain	5.95	Free	Unlimited	Yes	Yes	Unlimited
Easy CGI	7.96	Free	350 GB	Yes	V. limited	500
Webhosting- pad	1.99	Free	Unlimited	Yes	Yes	Unlimited
Doteasy basic	Free	25/yr	100 MB	Yes	Limit- ed	10
Doteasy unlimited	9.95	25/yr	20 GB	Yes	Yes	

Print Services Comparison Chart

Company	Business cards	Brochures	Fliers	News-letters	Shipping Time
UPrinting	250/$20.89	500/$64.17	500/$64.17	n/a	3 Days
Printplace	250/$15.50	250/$162.50	250/$162.50	n/a	5 Days
Overnight Prints	250/$24.95	100/$99.95	n/a	n/a	Varies
Printing for less	500/$48.45	250/$268.50	n/a	250/ $267.25	4 Days
Printrunner	250/$19.95	250/$164.96	250/$109.95	500/ $435.60	4 Days
Printing You Can Trust	n/a	500/$202.80	n/a	500/ $570.33	
Vistaprint	250/$14.99	250/$112.49	250? $100.99	n/a	Varies

Pet Sitting Insurance Comparison

Pet Sitter Associates:

Cost: $174/yr for first member

Each additional covered person
+$80 each

Prerequisites: none

Coverage: 2,000,000 Annual Aggregate
$1,000,000 Each Occurrence
$5000 Medical Expense
$1,000,000 Personal/Ad Inj
$2,000,000 Products/ Completed Ops
$100,000 Fire
$5000 Medical
$2000 Lost/stolen key
$1000 Each vet expense (no liability necessary)
$5000 Aggregate Vet Expense
$10,000 CCC/Animal Bailee

Coverage for damage to client's property is <u>optional</u>.
You must add the optional 'Special Properly of Others"
to cover things like accidental breakage or damage to
the *client's property* (such as household items) caused
by you / your children / employees & ICs.
(+ $100, listed above

Deductible: No deductible for claims, EXCEPT $500
per incident IF you purposely took an animal outdoors:

Not on a leash, outside of it's own "above ground fence that will keep pets inside and people and other animals outside"

Not on a leash, inside of any unfenced yard

Not on a leash, inside of any invisible fence.

Business Insurers of the Carolinas:

Cost: $274-$499 base rate
for individual policy.
Starting at $325
base rate for standard policy (covers multiple employees, and rates dependent on gross income).

Prerequisites: Must be PSI or NAPPS Member

Coverage: $2,000,000 Annual Aggregate
$1,000,000 Each Occurrence
$5000 Medical Expense
$1,000,000 Personal/ Ad Inj
$1,000,000 Prd/Completed Ops
$100,000 Fire
$2500 Lost Key
$10,000+ CCC/Animal Bailee

Coverage for damage to client's property is included.

Deductible: $100 per claim, all claims

Kennel Pro Insurance:

Cost: Several plans available. There is a $350 base rate. Other plans offered are the Platinum Package, and the Gold Package for kennels.

Prerequisites: none

Coverage: 4,000,000 Aggregate
$2,000,000 Each Occurrence
$5000 Medical Expense
$2,000,000 Personal/Ad Inj
$4,000,000 Prd/Completed Ops
$300,000 Fire to rented premise
$10,000 Medical Expenses
$10,000 CCC/Animal Bailee

Pet Sitting Associations Comparative Charts

Professional United Pet Sitters
$29.94 for Lifetime Membership
Directory Listing Member-ship to Forums & Links Boards. email forwarding alias of your choice @petsits. com Free Consultation or Form Customization / Logo insertion. Professional, Customizable Pet Sitting / Dog Walking / Pet Care Business Forms & Marketing Materials Budgeting, Mileage, Financial, Estimating and Scheduling Tool Workbook Pet Sitting Information, Marketing, Website, Startup, and other Guides List of 75+ Pet Service Directory listing sites (most listings free!), and other money saving pet supply links. Pet Recipes

Pet Sitters International
$140 per Year $5.00 extra to receive membership renewal by mail $7.50 for membership certificate
Directory Listing Health Insurance Discounts Discounted Background Checks Downloadable Templates and Resources Discounted Website Creation and Hosting Member Discount Programs Pet sitter Networking Registration Discount on All PSI Store Online Merchandise Trade Magazine Accreditation Program Annual Conferences Regional Meetings Teleconferences Monthly e-communication Member Forum & Member Support Staff

National Association of Professional Pet Sitters
$160 per Year for sole proprietors $500 per year for corporations and LLC's
Website Listing Discounted Trade Conference Certification Program Business Forms Discount on Credit card processing Discounted e-zine Discounted Business Insurance Discounted Background Check Mentoring Teleconferences Chat List Discounted Educational Library Quarterly Magazine PR Support Business Guides Presents for Pets Program, School Program Legislation Information

Pet Care Services Association
$1500 for Lifetime Member-ship
Directory listing
Trade Magazine
E-Newsletter
Discounts on Pet Care Classes
Accreditation Program
Annual Convention
Staples "Business Advantage" Discount Program
Discounted Health, Life, and Disability Insurance

Samples

The following samples were created by Spot Check Pet Services. The company information has been removed and replaced with the words "your company, your tagline, and ___," where appropriate.

Marketing Materials

Samples include:

- Price menu
- Door Hanger
- Thanksgiving Postcard
- Apartment Move-in Coupon

COMPANY NAME

tagline

SERVICES

DAILY PET VISITS & DOG WALKS

Daily pet visits are designed to ease the stress of your absence during the long work day. Each visit includes such value added services as brushing, checking food and water, and cleaning up any "accidents" which may have occurred in the house, along with a nice leisurely walk. We'll even give you a "daily report" spotlighting anything of interest which occurs while we're with your pet. That way you'll feel like you're right there with your pal!. Discount for two visits per day. Substantial discount for monthly booking.

$___ - ___

PUPPY VISITS

For puppies and young dogs, we will visit twice daily, providing that extra attention babies need. We will work on basic obedience, such as leash training, name recognition, and simple commands like "Sit!," and "\stay." We will provide you with daily progress reports and tips for continuing with the lessons.

$___ each visit

PET SITTING

Whether called away for business or pleasure, you can feel secure in the knowledge that your pet is comfortable and well cared for in the security of his own home environment. We will visit morning and evening, providing all the services listed in daily pet visits, plus we'll bring in the mail and newspapers, turn your lights on/off, water plants, open and close blinds, and any other basic tasks you might require.

$___ per day for dogs, or $___ per day for cats. Rates may be different for multiple pet homes

PET TAXI/PET FOOD DELIVERY SERVICE

The demands of today's busy lifestyle don't always accommodate pet lovers needs. Let us do the driving for you! We will make sure your pet makes it to all scheduled appointments on time, or if you're running low on pet food, we'll deliver your preferred brand right to your door, giving you that extra time to spend enjoying your pet.

$___ for taxi

Supply delivery fee is $___ plus the cost of items.

WEEKLY PET WASTE REMOVAL

Pet waste is not only unpleasant and smelly, it also poses health risks to humans and animals alike, as well as damaging lawns and contaminating water. Leave the cleanup to us, and you can have a pleasant and healthy outdoor experience, as well as some well deserved free time to spend doing more enjoyable tasks.

Price varies by yard size and number of pets, usually between $___ and $___ per month

Mileage surcharges apply to some in-town areas, and all areas outside of _____.

Phone: (___)___-____
Website: www._____.com
Email: _____@_____.com

CUT OUT
FOR DOOR
HANGER.

Spot Check Pet Services

We're man's best friends best friends!

Spot Check Pet Services offers premium pet care solutions for San Antonio's busy pet lovers.

You can count on us to be there for your best friend when you aren't able!

Fully Insured and Member of Pet Sitter Associates, LLC

*Daily Visits and Walks: *$___*

*Twice Daily Puppy Visits: *$___*

*Pet Sitting: *$___ per day*

*Pet Taxi: *$___ r/t*

*Pet Food Delivery: *please call*

*Weekly Pet Waste Removal: *price depends on yard size and number of pets, usually between $___ and $___ per month*

Initial consultation is always Free!

Call today, your pet's will thank you!

(___) ___-_____
or you can visit us on the web at:

www._____.com

Company name

tagline

Don't forget to make reservations for your Thanksgiving pet care needs. Your pets will thank you!

Phone:
Web:
Email:

Call now to ensure availability
Mention this card to waive the
holiday surcharge.

Community: _____

Courtesy of (Leasing Agent) _____   Expires _____

10% off first visit

Spot Check Pet Services

We're man's best friend!

San Antonio's premier pet care solutions provider for today's busy lifestyles

(___) ___-_____
www._____.com

This coupon entitles the bearer to a 10% discount on either their first month of daily visit service or any pet sitting booking of 4 or more days in length.

This generous savings is brought to you courtesy of your caring Apartment Community Staff

Not redeemable for cash.
Redemption value not to exceed $90.00

Compassionate Pet Care

Administrative Materials

Monthly Profit/Loss Spreadsheet

Month: Year:

Income Summary for:

	Week 1	Week 2	Week 3	Week 4	Week 5	Total
Pet Sitting						
Pet Taxi						
Delivery						
Bathing						
Advertising						
Admin						
Phones						
Insurance						
Dues						
Website						
Misc						
Total						

Miles	
Vehicle 1	
Vehicle 2	
Total	
Deductible	
amount	

Total Profit/Loss

Three Year Profit/Loss Spreadsheet

3 YEAR FINANCIAL STATEMENT   2007   2008   2009   Total

MONTH	2007	2008	2009	Total
JANUARY				
FEBRUARY				
MARCH				
APRIL				
MAY				
JUNE				
JULY				
AUGUST				
SEPTEMBER				
OCTOBER				
NOVEMBER				
DECEMBER				
TOTAL				

Correspondence

Apartment Leasing Agent Promotional Letter

Dear Leasing Staff,

 I see that your apartment complex accepts pets. I would like to take the opportunity to offer my pet care services to your community. Our services are beneficial not only to your residents, but also to your staff and property as well.

The benefits to your residents are:

New residents will not know anyone when they first move in, so they won't have any neighborhood friends to ask to look after their pets if they need to take a trip, have an emergency arise, or work long hours and need their dog taken out midday. We provide professional care for a wide variety of pets, and are fully insured and experienced. A 10% introductory discount will be given to all new customers you refer to us.

The benefits of our pet care to you are:

Daily walks will help insure that residents' pets relieve themselves outside during the long workday, helping keep carpet stains and smells down. Another added benefit for your community is that we always clean up pet waste when we walk our client's dogs, so there'll be less mess for your grounds maintenance staff to take care of!

I am enclosing an informational brochure to explain all the great services that we offer to pet lovers, along with a flier outlining my referral program in which you'll receive a

$5.00 "finders fee" for any new customers you send booking 4 or more days of pet sitting or weekly services. I would appreciate your help in getting the word out about the fantastic services available to them. If you'd like additional brochures to include with new resident packets, please let me know!

Thanks again!

Sincerely,

P.S. Please keep us in mind for your own pet care needs, to help your pets through those long days, or when you travel for business or pleasure!

Apartment Locator Promotional Letter

Dear Locators,

I would like to take the opportunity to offer my pet care services to your customers. Our services are beneficial not only to residents, but also to the staff and properties you work with as well.

The benefits to residents are:

New residents will not know anyone when they first move in, so they won't have any neighborhood friends to ask to look after their pets if they need to take a trip, have an emergency arise, or work long hours and need their dog taken out midday. We provide professional care for a wide variety of pets, and are fully insured and experienced. A 10% introductory discount will be given to all new customers you refer to us.

The benefits to apartment communities:

Daily walks will help insure that residents' pets relieve themselves outside during the long workday, helping keep carpet stains and smells down. Another added benefit for communities is that we always clean up pet waste when we walk our client's dogs, so there'll be less mess for grounds maintenance staff to take care of!

I am enclosing an informational brochure to explain all the great services that we offer to pet lovers, along with a flier outlining my referral program in which you'll receive a $5.00 "finders fee" for any new customers you send booking 4 or more days of pet sitting or weekly services. I would appreciate your help in getting the word out about the fantastic services available to them. If you'd like additional brochures to give to prospective residents, please let me know!

Thanks again!

Sincerely,

P.S. Please keep us in mind for your own pet care needs, to help your pets through those long days, or when you travel for business or pleasure!

Real Estate Agent Promotional Letter

_____, Realty/Locater
Address 1
Address 2
San Antonio, TX 78###

Dear _____,

My name is _____, and I am the owner of _____.
_____ is _____ premier professional pet care
solutions provider. We offer daily walks, pet sitting, pet
food and supply delivery, pet taxi, and pet waste removal to
San Antonio and surrounding areas

I know that you will come in contact with many pet owners
in the course of your work, all of which will become new to
their neighborhoods, with your help. They won't have any
neighborhood friends to ask to look after their pets if they
need to take a trip, or have an emergency arise. Pet sitting
and pet care are valuable services to animal lovers, and you
can help connect your clients with reliable services!

I am sending you an informational brochure to explain all
the great services that I am offering to pet lovers, along
with a flier outlining my referral program in which you'll
receive a $5.00 "finders fee" for any new customers you
send booking 4 or more days of pet sitting. I would
appreciate your help in getting the word out about the
fantastic services available to them.

Thanks again!

Sincerely,

P.S. Please keep us in mind for your own pet care needs, to help your pets through those long days, or when you travel for business or pleasure!

Brochure Request Response Letter

Name
Address
City, State Zip

Date

Dear _____,

Thank you for your inquiry about our pet sitting
services. As promised, here is a brochure briefly
detailing our services and fees. As a thank you for
becoming a new customer, I am also enclosing a
coupon worth 10% off of your first booking with us.

The following e-mail addresses are references you
may contact regarding my services. Both are cat
lovers, and have been with me for a very long time.
I hope you will find this information helpful:

_____

_____

Also, if you have any additional questions relating
to my insurance coverage, you may find information
at _____. My member number is _____.
There is an informative f.a.q. page detailing the
policy, as well as the additional personal property
rider we discussed.

Please don't hesitate to let me know if you have any
other questions. You may reach me by phone at

(210) _____, or by e-mail at _____.com. I look forward to serving your pet care needs!

Sincere thanks,

Enc

Collection Letter

Date

Name
Address
City, State Zip

Dear _____,

We sincerely enjoyed caring for _____ for you during
your trip from _____. It is our hope that we will be able to
provide services to you in the future, should you need us.

As stated in the first line of our Legal Considerations Contract,
we do require payment be made within 3 days of the final visit.
Unfortunately, we have yet to receive remittance for the
services performed.

Pet care is not only our passion it is our profession. We count
on prompt payments from our valued customers to support our
family. As we are certain this is simply an oversight on your
part, we are waiving the late fees at this time. However, if
payment is not received by _____, we will be forced to
assess charges as outlined in line 1 of the Legal Considerations
Contract.

Please feel free to contact us with any questions or concerns
you may have. I am enclosing a duplicate bill and a return
envelope for your convenience.

Thank you,

Enc.

Useful Websites

Organizations

Small Business Administration
www.sba.gov

Professional United Pet Sitters
www.petsits.com

National Association of Professional Pet Sitters
www.petsitters.org

Pet Sitters International
www.petsit.com

Pet Sitters Associates
www.petsitllc.com

Online Pet Sitter Directories

Pet-Sitters Biz—Listings are $24 per year
www.pet-sitters.biz

Pet Sitting Directory—Listings are $34.95 per year for standard listing, or $56.95 per year for premier listings
www.petsittingdirectory.com

Pet Sitter Directory—Listings are free with reciprocal link, or $14.95 per year
www.petsitterdirectory.com

Pet Sit USA—Listings are $36 per year
www.petsitusa.com

Pet Sitter Portal—Listings are $9.99 per year for basic, or $19.99 per year for deluxe listings
www.petsitterportal.com

Pet Sit Center—Listings are $20 per year
www.petsitcenter.com

Find a Pet Sitter
www.findapetsitter.net

Planet Pets—listings are free for the first 90 days; $4 per month thereafter for a basic listing. Upgraded listings are $8 per month, and video ads are $247 for the 1st year and $19.99 per month thereafter.
www.planetpets.com

Other directories include:

www.homeandpetsitters.com
www.findapetsitter.net

www.petsitter.com
www.sitercity.com
www.petcaretakers.com

Online Search Engine Submission Sites for Websites

www.addme.com/submission/free-submission-start.php

www.google.com/addurl

www.submitexpress.com

www.addpro.com

www.website-hit-counters.com/free-website-submission.html

www.evrsoft.com/fastsubmit

www.buildtraffic.com/indexnew.shtml

www.startranking.com

www.nexcomp.com/weblaunch

www.websitesubmit.hypermart.net

www.myfreeseo.com

www.buildtraffic.net

www.submitsolution.com

www.ineedhits.com

www.submitasite.com

www.100keywords.com

www.freeaddurl.org

www.netmechanic.com

www.quickregister.net

www.dynamicsubmission.com

www.hit-counter-download.com/free-search-engine-submission.html

www.trafficzap.com/searchsubmit.php

Online Office Supplies

www.officedepot.com

www.staples.com

www.officemax.com

www.thegreenoffice.com

www.quill.com

www.officesupply.etc.com

www.discountedofficesupply.com

www.reliable.com

www.buyonlinenow.com

Printing Services

www.uprinting.com

www.printplace.com

www.overnightprints.com

www.printingforless.com

www.printrunner.com

www.printingyoucantrust.com

www.vistaprint.com

Free Online Computer Program Tutorials

www.fgcu.edu/support/office2000/index.html

www.brainybetty.com

www.baycongroup.com

http://office.microsoft.com/en-us/training

www.ingramcontent.com/pod-product-compliance
Lightning Source LLC .
Chambersburg PA
CBHW072035190526
45165CB00017B/883